Strategic Default

How to Create a Brighter Financial Future
For You, Your Family, or Your Business

ISBN: 978-1-60910-420-7

Dedication

I would like to dedicate this book to my wife Mable for being with me through difficult times and great times.

Strategic Default

How to Create a Brighter Financial Future
For You, Your Family, or Your Business

By

A. A. Diji

Disclaimer

The author and publisher have used their best efforts in preparing this book. They make no representations or warranties of any kind with respect to this book or its contents. The author and publisher disclaim all such representations and warranties, including for example financial advice for a particular purpose. The author and the publisher are not financial advisors and they are not acting in the capacity of a financial advisor.

The advice and strategies contained herein may not be suitable for your situation. The author and publisher are not engaged in rendereing legal, financial, or professional advice. Law and practices often vary from state to state and if legal or other professional assistance is required, the services of a professional should be sought. This book is not a substitute for competent professional advice when and where appropriate.

Except as specifically stated in this book, neither the author or publisher, nor any authors, contributors, or other representatives will be liable for damages arising out of or in connection with the use of this book. This is a comprehensive limitation of liability that applies to all damages of any kind, including but not limited to special, incidental, consequential, or other damages.

Contents

Forewords

There is no doubt that we are in the midst of the worst financial upheaval the United States has experienced since the Great Depression.

In order to take advantage of, and not become victim to, the changes in our economy requires a significant change in the way you think about and act on the information you receive about wealth and the economy. It requires the mindset of a business owner or investor to see the great opportunity that this economy presents to realign your assets and reposition yourself by unloading worthless, money wasting, debt laden assets and accumulate valued assets at a discount. It requires you to do the math; cut costs and increase income. When the numbers no longer add up in your favor and the probability of a turn around is low, you simply cease to expend another resource (time, energy, money) into that asset. You stop wasting resources on a "nonperforming asset" and realign your assets to work for you in a new opportunity.

You can continue to do what you have been doing for the past several years; dumping money into a 401K, trying to gain appreciation and borrow against equity in your home, putting cash in the bank, etc., all of the post Depression strategies for gaining personal wealth or you can accept that the world as we know it has changed forever, and therefore the methods we used to create and preserve wealth must change along with it.

In this new economy, I encourage you to reevaluate where you are putting every penny. Where you can cut costs, defer payments, renegotiate price or terms, or simply eliminate the expense – do so immediately in order to free up your money for realignment into new investment opportunities.

The ultimate difference as to which side you find yourself during this economic return will be based upon whether or not you reposition yourself and understand where you find yourself in the great ideological divide. To the wise and brave that read this book, do the math and take action to save themselves from certain stress and financial loss by realigning your assets, I applaud you.

Heru Ur-Nekhet, President
Insiders Group, Inc.
www.insidersgroup.com
New York May 2010

❋

I can remember when I told the author, A. A. Diji, about my belief in the imminent collapse of mortgage lenders and financial institutions. My financial research of American Home Mortgage confirmed its business model was based on nothing but air. American Home Mortgage filed for bankruptcy in August 2007. It was the 10th largest home loan lender at the time. American Home Mortgage was not heavily involved in subprime mortgages. It provided loans to borrowers with high credit scores aka Alt-A loans. As a former Wall Street stockbroker, current real estate investor and an owner of a prominent New York City real estate brokerage, I knew that there was something wrong with mortgages loans made from 2005 to 2008. I witnessed firsthand many first-time homebuyers and investors obtaining financing with good credit alone. These buyers purchased properties with No Income, No

Asset verification loans, 90% to 100% loan-to-value loans, 3 to 5 year fixed adjustable-rate mortgages, and negative amortization loans. Lenders were all too ready to lend since each loan represented a significant profit. The profit did not come from lenders keeping the loan on its books, rather each and every closed loan was later sold to a Wall Street investment bank to be later repackaged into a collateral debt security with a thousand other loans.

If there was one thing I learned as a stock broker, it was "everything that goes up must come down". It reminded me of the savings and loans debacle. It was like the "dot com" implosion. I explained my observations and concerns to Diji. As a real estate attorney, investor, and broker, Diji began an earnest quest to learn more about the true consequences of re-packaging loans into securities. Each week, I received a phone call or email about how all types of loans, including school loans, auto loans, and credit card loans, were turned into collateral debt obligations, derivatives, commercial and residential mortgage backed securities, credit default swaps, and other "exotic" instruments developed by Wall Street. I learned that the financial industry was living in a house of cards that involved consumers, governments, businesses, and banks. Everyone and everything was in deep debt like never before. Of course none of this surprised me. Yet at some point I believed Diji had become overly obsessed about the whole thing. Well, it's a good thing he did. His obsession eventually led to this important book. Thankfully, it is one of the few times I have seen an unyielding obsession turn into a positive result.

Gordon Sokich, CEO
Luxor Homes & Investment Realty, LLC
www.luxornyc.com
New York June 2010

Introduction

If you are among the millions of people in the United States and around the world who owe a significant debt (most likely a home mortgage, but even a credit card or business debt) and are concerned about the drain on your cash flow and savings as the result of that debt, this book is for you.

Let's say you bought a house for $350,000 and took out a mortgage for $300,000. Ordinarily, over the years your house would gradually appreciate in value—say, to $400,000. This is the value that you are receiving in exchange for your mortgage of $300,000. And it's fair. You know that if something happened and you could not pay your mortgage, you could sell the house for $400,000, pay off your mortgage, and even make a profit. This is the way the world is supposed to work, isn't it? If you are an adult, you know that it's the way the world worked for our parents and grandparents. You bought a house and the house appreciated in value as you paid off your mortgage over ten or twenty or thirty years.

But suppose your house depreciated in value. Suppose that after a major recession you discover that you are paying a mortgage of $300,000 for a house that is only worth $200,000. If you sold your house on the open market you would not even recoup the outstanding balance on your mortgage. You would have no house and you would owe your mortgage lender $100,000! Suddenly you have no equity in the house you think you own. In such a case, your mortgage is deep "underwater" and you have no life preserver.

Faced with a house that is worth less than your mortgage, what are your choices? If you can make your mortgage payments, one choice would be to sit tight and pray that you remained healthy long enough to see real estate prices rise again (as they surely will; the only question is how long will it take?). Eventually your underwater home would regain its value and emerge from its watery grave.

If you cannot make your mortgage payments, or if you expect to move, or if you are in ill health, or if you simply cannot stomach the idea of paying an inflated price for your home, then you need to consider your exit strategy. You need to consider how you are going to fix your problem.

You have a variety of options. You can apply for a federal home loan modification program. You can ask your bank to modify your loan (good luck on that one!). You can ask your lender about a short sale. You can voluntarily give the property to the lender. You can declare bankruptcy.

You can also walk away from your debt. This is called a *strategic default*. The word "strategic" is used because you are deliberately taking this action to accomplish a specific goal. You're not defaulting because you have no other choice; this is something that you are choosing to do.

For many of us, this idea seems vaguely immoral. After all, isn't a contract a binding agreement? Isn't there personal honor involved?

Yes and no. Strategic defaults are commonly used by wealthy individuals and corporations who are concerned with one thing: the bottom line. Yes, it is good to honor one's obligations, but it is foolish to put oneself in harm's way to do it. If your home is underwater, you know that you are one accident or one serious illness away from disaster. You know that the spirit in which you signed your mortgage has been violated. You know that if you keep to your agreement, your lender will pocket a sum of money that far exceeds the current value of your home. Using the money you pay, your lender can go out and buy a bigger house, or even two houses. But you are stuck.

And then there's the frustration of knowing that while you are paying your mortgage of $300,000, for only $200,000 you could buy a house identical to the one you are now living in. In fact, someone else probably will. And they will use their extra cash to vacation in Europe or pay for their kids' college educations. Your extra cash will go to straight into your lender's giant piggy bank.

Remember the words of oil baron J. Paul Getty: "If I owe the bank $100, that's my problem. If I owe the bank $100 million, that's the bank's problem." What this means is that a loan agreement is a deal between two parties. Like it or not, the lender assumes some risk. One of the risks assumed by a lender is that over time, conditions will change and the borrower will become increasingly unable or unwilling to pay. And that can be a problem for the lender.

Strategic Default will show you what you can do to fix your problem. We'll review the choices that you have. We'll discuss the pros and cons of strategic default, examine how it has been used and by whom, and why it has become an acceptable alternative. You'll understand the legal risks and the inevitable change to your credit rating. If you choose to proceed with a strategic default, we'll guide you through the process. We'll provide steps, tools, and proper consideration for an effective strategic default.

We'll reveal how you can move ahead with your life and rebuild your credit and enjoy the peace and tranquility of a life without the looming burden of valueless debt. The ultimate goals are cash flow protection, savings preservation, and wealth protection. In the end, we all have the right to choose the path we take, being aware of both the potential consequences and the expected rewards. This book will help you on your journey along the path you choose.

1. Who This Book Is For

In the United States and around the world a financial crisis is affecting people, businesses, and even governments. The crisis is devastating rich and poor alike, families, individuals, the young and the old.

Across the income spectrum, for individuals the primary financial problem is burdensome debt, particularly real estate debt and credit card debt.

Many people are heavily leveraged and are seeking a way out. It is true that during the previous decades, credit was cheap. Many people borrowed more than they should have. They assumed—falsely—that their homes would continue to appreciate in value and that somehow their mounting debts could be paid back. They built houses of cards that the strong winds of the recession blew apart.

The innocent suffer along with the guilty. Many borrowers were duped by overzealous or even unethical mortgage lenders. They signed adjustable-rate mortgages and then got hit with exorbitant rate increases. Other homeowners bought at the top of the market and then saw the value of their homes plummet through no fault of their own.

Traditionally, one of the greatest forms of wealth comes from real estate ownership, but that has changed. It is now estimated that in the past three years a trillion dollars of real estate wealth has evaporated. Individuals and investors own properties with unaffordable mortgage payments that have principle balances greater than the value of the property.

The credit markets have dried up. Financial institutions are not extending credit unless the borrower meets a strict set of criteria. In order to obtain a loan, one must have excellent credit, verifiable income, and substantial cash reserves. This is a tall order for many people and businesses alike.

How can you survive in this toxic financial environment?

If you are reading this book, then you are concerned about your debts. You may be either unable to pay your debts, such as your mortgage or credit cards, or you believe that to continue to pay for something that has lost its value is simply not a sound financial decision.

Even if you can afford to make your payments you may be seriously considering stopping payments on one or more of your loans. In other words, you are contemplating walking away from your debt. This is called *strategic default.*

A strategic default is a financial decision to not make any more loan payments even if you have the money to do so.

There are three primary goals of a strategic default:

1. Cash Flow Protection.
2. Savings Preservation.
3. Wealth Protection.

There are other reasons to strategically default. A homeowner or debtor may strategically default in order to get a loan modification. A person may strategically default to use the available cash for another purpose. Another may strategically default to pile up as much cash as possible and walk away from the debt at the last minute.

A recent study of homeowners found that when equity shortfall reached 50% of the value of their house, 17% of borrowers would default, even if they could afford to pay their mortgage.[i]

You may decide to strategically default for any of the following reasons:

- You are concerned about your financial future. There is a real fear that you will have less cash, lower net worth, and less retirement savings in the long term if you continue to pay.
- You have no immediate concern about the damage to your credit.
- You do not have any desire to obtain more credit or purchase any item requiring credit.
- You want to see an increase in your cash flow by not paying your debt, by settling principle balances for less than what is owed, and/or by collecting income from tenants or customers.
- You seek to gain an upper hand in negotiating with a lender for a modified loan since most lenders will not agree to modify a loan if the payments are current.
- You have carefully considered the strategy. From a pure business perspective the risks are significantly outweighed by the reward.
- Your mortgage is underwater or upside-down or has negative equity. They all mean the same thing. In other words your mortgage debt is greater than the value of your property. You choose not to pump money into an asset that has become a liability.
- You seek to live in a property, collect rent, or hold onto an asset as long as possible to pile up cash.

Traditionally (and this is what the U.S. government is advocating), homeowners who are under mortgage pressure try to get their loan modified. They appeal to the creditor for a forbearance or a lower interest rate or permission to skip a month and tack the payment on at the end. However, most lenders require some form of default and hardship from a borrower before agreeing to modify a loan.

The reality is this: If a borrower continues to stay current with their loan, their lender will not provide better loan terms. Under such conditions the lender has absolutely no incentive to take money out of its own pocket (can you blame them?). But if a borrower decides to risk a bad credit rating and stops paying the loan for a month or two or three, their lender is forced to respond and may even provide better loan terms.

Which path would you choose?

The Key Issue: Your Credit Score

In the minds of most people, there are three main barriers to strategic default:

1. Social Stigma and Moral Issues.
2. Fear of the Consequences.
3. Damage to Your Credit Rating.

We'll address the first two issues, *social stigma and morality* and *perceived consequences,* later in the book. You will see that in the business world these concerns have never been a problem. In law school, they teach students that a contract (such as a mortgage loan or credit card account) is an agreement between two parties. If one party (you) breaks the agreement, there is a penalty. That's all. There is no moral component. You are not robbing a bank or mugging an old lady. A strategic default is a business decision and nothing more.

The third issue, your credit rating, deserves serious thought. We will start at the beginning: our obsession with credit and our credit rating. When did this begin? Many analysts can pinpoint an exact date: in September of 1958, Bank of America in Fresno, California launched its pioneering BankAmericard credit card program.[ii] It was the first attempt to create an all-purpose credit card, and within a decade millions of credit cards were in use in America. At the same time there arose the need to measure individual consumer creditworthiness. In the 1970s the development of computerized data processing led to the rise of the big three credit bureaus: Experian, TransUnion, and Equifax. These giants popularized the personal credit score, and a generation of Americans was pummeled with the same message: *Don't Screw Up Your Credit Rating!* If you do, you will be miserable and poor and you won't be able to buy anything.

Well, yes and no. A credit score is a tool. A tool that does not need to be used every day. If you have a lousy credit score, it means that you may have trouble borrowing money. You may have trouble getting a mortgage or a car loan or another credit card.

But what if you don't care about your credit score?

Do you plan to buy anything on credit anytime soon? A credit score is important to those who need access to credit. If you don't need access to credit, it's a meaningless number.

And besides, a negative event on your credit score doesn't last forever. A mortgage default can remain on your credit history for seven years. Not a moment longer. After seven years, it's as if it never happened. And even during that seven years, as the event ages it can lose importance.

If you are willing to live without access to credit for a few years, you are okay with the moral and social issues and you are making a business decision for your financial future and well being, then you are ready to plan your strategic default.

2. What Is Strategic Default?

An increasing number of people have decided to intentionally stop making mortgage loan payments, even if they can afford to do so. They have decided to make a strategic default.

For individuals, strategic default is most often associated with home mortgage loans. However, strategic default is a tool used for credit card debt, business loans, home equity lines of credit, and personal loans.

Generally, the primary rationale for a strategic default is economic. Moral, emotional, and social issues can complicate the decision to stop making loan payments even if the money is available. These moral, emotional, and social issues intersect with an individual's "rational" decision to stop losing money. Our society generally places a strong taboo against breaking an agreement, and there may be social costs to consider when an individual decides to abandon a property and stop making mortgage payments.

A property owner normally considers a strategic default when the value of the property is below the mortgage balance due a lender. There is a corresponding concern that monthly mortgage loan payments will become a permanent drain of available cash savings with little chance of recovering the loss. The rationale is that it does not make economic sense to make mortgage loan payments on a property that has no equity or any hope of gaining equity.

Forms of Strategic Default

When faced with valueless debt, particularly an underwater mortgage, you can consider a variety of options. Some are more drastic than others, and you may want to try a softer approach before getting into a full-blown strategic default.

Loan Workout, Restructure, or Modification

A loan modification is when a lender agrees to modify the terms of a loan because the debtor can establish a financial hardship. Generally, a lender will require a hardship letter and financial information in order to establish the borrower's inability to make current payments.

For homeowners, the federal government has created the Making Home Affordable Program. Within this umbrella program, which is administered by the Department of Housing and Urban Development (HUD), there are several programs designed to help distressed homeowners. They include:

• **The Home Affordable Modification Program (HAMP)**, provides eligible homeowners the opportunity to modify their mortgages to make them more affordable.[iii] The goal is to help three to four million U.S. homeowners by 2012. On March 26, 2010, the Obama Administration announced expanded flexibility for mortgage servicers to assist more unemployed homeowners and homeowners who are underwater through the program. The program originally was deemed a failure because lender participation was voluntary; but the new version has teeth and most lenders are required to participate.

• **The Second Lien Modification Program (2MP)** offers homeowners a way to modify their second mortgages to make them more affordable when their first mortgage is modified under HAMP.

• **The Home Affordable Refinance Program (HARP)** gives homeowners with loans owned or guaranteed by Fannie Mae or Freddie Mac an opportunity to refinance into more affordable monthly payments.

• **The Home Affordable Foreclosure Alternatives Program (HAFAP)** provides opportunities for homeowners who can no longer afford to stay in their home but want to avoid foreclosure to transition to more affordable housing through a short sale or deed-in-lieu of foreclosure.

If you do not qualify for any of the above-mentioned programs, then a lender may have an "in-house" program. All loan modification programs are intended for homeowners who can demonstrate financial hardship. If you can't do that, then it is unlikely you will qualify for any of the programs.

Deed in Lieu of Foreclosure

Essentially, a deed in lieu of foreclosure is when a bank agrees to take a property back to pay off the mortgage. This means there is no foreclosure. It simply becomes a written agreement between you and the bank.

Short Sale

There are some lenders willing to accept a lump sum or balloon payment that is less than the full amount due on a mortgage loan. This is commonly referred to as a *short sale*. Basically, with the prior knowledge and approval of your lender, you sell your house for a fair market price and give your lender all the proceeds.

A short sale becomes an option when you are behind in your mortgage payments or your lender has begun foreclosure proceedings. The benefit to you is that it ends the foreclosure process. It also keeps further derogatory information from being placed on the credit report. A lender must approve a short sale in writing before a property can be sold. A lender benefits from a short sale because it can minimize its losses in a falling market.

The lender will appraise the property. They may also request a listing agreement from a licensed broker. A listing agreement tells the bank that the owner tried to sell the property. The lender will want financial information from the owner/borrower, information about the property, and the exact terms of any short sale deal. The lender needs to see a written contract between the owner and the buyer to make sure the owner isn't walking away with any cash from the deal. Some lenders may allow a payment of moving expenses to a seller.

For a short sale, the bottom line is the same as a loan modification: your lender will not talk to you unless forced to. If you are current in your payments and have no immediate financial hardship, your lender has no incentive to consider a short sale. Why should they when you are dutifully sending them your mortgage check every month?

A Note About Deficiency

In most forms of settlement of mortgage debt where the property is underwater, there will be a deficiency that must be resolved. For example, if a property owner owes the lender $400,000 and the lender agrees to sell the property for $350,000, the deficiency is $50,000.

If the lender forgives the deficiency then the property owner can be taxed on this $50,000 deficiency, because the Internal Revenue Service (IRS) believes that since you received a loan of $400,000 and paid back $350,000, then $50,000 is still in your pocket as income. Currently, there is a contravening law that protects you from federal taxation. The Mortgage Forgiveness Debt Relief Act of 2007[iv] established a 3-year moratorium (now extended to December 2012 by the Emergency Economic Stabilization Act of 2008) that prevents any debt forgiven by a lender from being counted as income by the IRS.

In some cases the lender will sue the homeowner personally for the deficiency. The most important principle is resolving the deficiency. Make sure that the deed is exchanged in full satisfaction of the outstanding debt. If the lender is unwilling to accept the deed in full satisfaction of the outstanding debt then make sure the lender agrees to forgive the deficiency.

Bankruptcy

If you are in financial distress and cannot pay your mortgage, you may consider filing for bankruptcy. The federal government has designed various programs or "chapters" designed for individuals, farms, businesses, and government entities. Chapter 7 is a liquidation of your assets, and is done under the administration of the U.S. Bankruptcy Court. It's the option available to individuals and businesses who have little or no income or cash flow. Chapter 13, also known as a "Wage Earner Bankruptcy," is a rehabilitation program that allows you to pay off your debts over time while you work. It also allows you to keep many of your assets. Filing either form of bankruptcy stops the foreclosure process and stops the activities of debt collectors.

Like loan modifications and short sales, bankruptcy is only for people in significant financial distress. In 2005, with the backing of major banks and credit card companies, the federal government tightened the requirements for bankruptcy.[v] (The credit card companies were displeased that so many customers were filing bankruptcy and not paying their enormous credit card bills.) To file bankruptcy you need to pass a stringent means test, and the penalties for fraudulently filing bankruptcy are severe.

Strategic Default

All of the debt relief options that we have reviewed are dependent upon one thing: that you are in demonstrable financial hardship.

But what if you are able to pay your mortgage, but with every check you write you cringe because you are paying an inflated price for a piece of property that you could buy today for far less? What if you see your cash being sucked into the greedy vortex of your mortgage, leaving you with nothing while your lender laughs all the way to the bank vault?

You have a choice: strategic default.

In its essence, strategic default is very simple. You just stop paying. And then you prepare for the consequences of not paying.

The primary consequences of not paying are:

1. Incurring a deficiency debt leading to a deficiency judgment.
2. Lower credit score.
3. Loss of the home or property to a foreclosure sale.
4. Aggressive debt collection tactics, including mail, letters, personal visits and lawsuits.

5. Recent government and financial industry actions against people who employ a strategic default.
6. Personal legal liability for unpaid debts.

As your plan unfolds, your lender will refuse to negotiate or your lender will agree to negotiate. If your lender refuses to negotiate then your house will eventually go into foreclosure and sold at an auction. Your other creditors can sue you for unpaid debts. If your lender agrees to negotiate then the outcome could be a settlemernt, short sale, deed-in-lieu, or a loan modification.

3. Who Has Used Strategic Default?

As you consider your choices, you may be concerned that by using a strategic default you are entering uncharted waters. You don't want to take a chance on a risky or unproven strategy. You need the assurance of knowing that your course of action has been done successfully by many others.

You can be assured that historically, strategic default has been employed by individuals, small businesses, corporations, and nations.

Corporations, which traditionally have operated more in the spirit of unvarnished self-interest than individuals, have long used various forms of strategic default to preserve capital. There are many corporations that have used bankruptcy primarily as a restricting method to force creditors into accepting lower payments.

A strategic default has been used by real estate investors to collect rental income. In an article from the therealdeal.com, one of New York City's largest real estate publications, Joshua Stein, chair of the education committee of the Mortgage Bankers Association of New York and a partner in the real estate practice group of Latham & Watkins, described it as a "famous technique for small-time real estate investors…[y]ou know you are going to lose the property, so... you put as much in your pocket as you can…during the last real estate downturn in the early 1990s, many investors were going into default and milking their properties for all the available cash."[vi] This is an example that many would question ethically: a landlord stops paying his mortgage but continues to collect rent, which he shovels into his bank account to extract as much value as possible from the failing asset. Not very nice, but it has been done more often than you might think.

Here's a more familiar, and defensible, example from the business world. In early 2009, Millenium Partners, the owner of the posh Four Seasons Hotel in San Francisco, faced a business downturn. The tourist industry had declined and hotels throughout California were going bankrupt. Millenium approached their mortgage loan servicer, LNR Property Corp., and requested a modification of their $90 million mortgage. LNR Property refused. According to the San Francisco *Business Times*, in June 2009, in an effort to force LNR Property to enter into negotiations, Millennium Partners "strategically withheld payment of debt service" on the loan.[vii] In October 2009, Millennium "submitted a proposal that the servicer deemed to be unacceptable," according to the credit-rating agency, Realpoint. The servicer then issued a notice of sale to proceed with the foreclosure.

Was Millenium greedy? Justifiably pragmatic? In 2009 a Realpoint analysis of the Four Seasons loan estimated that the value of the loan was only $55.7 million, over one-third less than the loan's $90 million value.

The story has an unexpected ending. Despite Millenium's high-stakes gambit, LNR Property didn't blink and didn't agree to a loan modification. In March 2010, Millennium announced that it had joined forces with private equity group Westbrook Partners and paid down the mortgage on the Four Seasons from $90 million to $55 million. Under the agreement Westbrook becomes two-thirds owner of the hotel while Millennium holds on to a one-third ownership interest and continues to manage the hotel. And so everyone goes home happy. The lesson is that while the outcome was not what anyone anticipated, the reality is that strategic default is a tool used by businesses that understand that anyone who lends money is exposed to risk that, when conditions demand, must be shared.

Here is another example. In May 2007, Morgan Stanley spent more than $2.5 billion on the purchase of ten office towers in San Francisco. The buildings were formerly owned by billionaire investor, Sam Zell's, Equity Office Properties and had been acquired by Blackstone Group LP earlier that year. Over the next two years, the properties lost fifty percent of their value. In December 2009, Morgan Stanley announced that it was giving back five of the buildings: One Post, 201 California St., Foundry Square I, 60 Spear St., and 188 Embarcadero.[viii]

Of course, Morgan Stanley hastened to insist that the return of the properties to Blackstone Group was not a strategic default. The bank negotiated an "orderly transfer" of the towers, said Alyson Barnes, a Morgan Stanley spokeswoman, in an interview with Bloomberg.com. "This isn't a default or foreclosure situation. We are going to give them the properties to get out of the loan obligation." If you tried the same thing with the McMansion you bought at the top of the market in 2007, you can bet that your lender would say that you were in default.

Material Adverse Effect

Some complex corporate loan documents contain a Material Adverse Effect clause. In legalese, Material Adverse Effect means an effect, event, development, or change that, individually or in the aggregate with all other effects, events, developments or changes, is materially adverse to the business, results of operations or physical or financial condition of the real property or improvements taken as a whole.

In plain English, this means that if the borrower can prove that business conditions have changed dramatically, and are not in the borrower's control, that the lender shall be compelled to agree to a modification. The recent credit and commercial real estate collapse prompted battalions of lawyers to scrutinize the fine print of many a loan agreement, searching for the elusive MAE clause.

Force Majeure

An Event of Force Majeure is "any act of God; war; riot; act of terrorism; embargo; governmental rule, regulation or decree; flood, fire, hurricane or other casualty; earthquake; strike, lockout, or other labor disturbance; the unavailability of labor or materials to the extent beyond the control of the party affected; or any other events or circumstances not within the reasonable control of the party affected, whether similar or dissimilar to any of the foregoing."

It was this principle that Donald Trump invoked when he wrangled with Deutsche Bank, to which he owed a balance of $334 million for the construction of Trump International Hotel and Tower in Chicago, which after the Sears Tower was to be the second-tallest building in that city.[ix]

Apparently construction was going well and condo sales were on track. Then the real estate market in Chicago plummeted. Trump wanted to delay construction until conditions improved and he asked Deutsche Bank to modify the loan. Deutsche Bank refused and demanded $40 million that Trump had personally guaranteed. Trump sued Deutsche, invoking force majeure and claimed that Deutsche had damaged his reputation. Trump cited a force majeure clause in the lending agreement that allows the borrower to postpone completion of the building if construction is delayed by events such as riots, floods, or strikes. He asserted that the great recession qualified as such an event.

A key element of Trump's argument was that he wanted to lower the prices on the unsold condominiums. Without a loan modification from Deutsche this would be impossible because Trump would be forced to absorb the loss. By refusing to grant him a delay on the outstanding payment, Trump argued that Deutsche was preventing him from lowering prices to meet the market level. When asked if the people who had already bought condos at the original price could get a discount too, Trump is said to have asserted that those folks were not covered by force majeure.

The Mortgage Bankers Association

If you are not yet convinced that strategic default is an accepted strategy used by corporations across America, consider the case of the Mortgage Bankers Association ("MBA"). This trade organization represents the interests of lenders. The Association's CEO, John Courson, has said that underwater borrowers should keep paying on their mortgage loans and should not walk away from lawful debts. In an interview, Courson invoked the morals clause and said, "What about the message they will send to their family and their kids and their friends?"

It's an understandable public stance. But when the chips were down, the MBA changed its tune. In 2007, the MBA decided that it needed to own its own headquarters building. The trade group's then-president, Jonathan Kempner, said, "We have come to the inescapable conclusion that owning our own building was the smartest long-term investment for the association." They bought a 10-story building in Washington, D.C., taking out a variable-rate mortgage loan for $79 million from PNC Financial Group.[x]

But as the economy soured the MBA had difficulty finding tenants for the building. In October 2009, the MBA told its members that they were getting out of the deal. The MBA said that continued ownership of the building would be "economically imprudent." In February 2010, the Co-Star

Group, Inc., announced that it had agreed to buy the MBA's building for $41.3 million.

So after owning their building for less than two years, the Mortgage Bankers Association bailed out and forced their lender to accept a *short sale* that took in half the amount of the mortgage. Why did PNC agree? The parties refused to release details of the agreement. But for the MBA it was a calculated business decision that they were very comfortable with.

Corporations, governments, and smart business people have employed strategic default for ages. However they have counted on everyday consumers to keep to their agreements to pay their debts—even if it is a struggle to do so. Average people have struggled because of emotional and moral reasons. The public has been conditioned to believe that debt must be paid at all costs. Current moral teachings, societal codes of conduct, and the law place a burden on individuals to pay their debts.

What is a mortgage or a credit card agreement? It is a contract between two parties. A dictionary definition of "contract" is this:

> **contract** 1) n. an agreement with specific terms between two or more persons or entities in which there is a promise to do something in return for a valuable benefit known as consideration.

"Consideration." Now there's the rub. When your house is deep underwater and you are paying every month for something that is grossly overvalued, you are not receiving due consideration.

Is this your lender's fault? Maybe; maybe not. It doesn't matter. All that matters is that you are not receiving due consideration.

The truth: "smart players" recognize that it does not make sense to destroy the future ability to earn or grow savings by sticking to a loan contract that can destroy financial well-being. Unfortunately everyday people did this and continue to do this all the time to their financial detriment. So if, like the good people of MBA, you are faced with the inescapable conclusion that your loan is "economically imprudent," do not fear to consider a strategic default.

4. Eleven Principles of Strategic Default

Before considering strategic default, you should develop a structured and carefully thought-out plan. In order to plan you should have in your mind a clear concept of the eleven principles of strategic default. With these principles established, you can move forward with confidence.

Here they are.

1. As Negative Equity Gets Worse, Strategic Default Looks Better

It's no secret that most rational people will not continue to make payments on a property or asset that has negative equity and has virtually no chance of gaining equity in the near future. Let's look at some examples.

Suppose you bought your home for $600,000 several years ago. Now your property is worth $450,000 and your mortgage balance is $500,000. Should the mortgage be paid? That's a tough question. Here are some of the pros and cons.

KEEP PAYING	DEFAULT
Property values will rise.	Property values will not rise, but not fast enough.
You plan on staying in your home with your family for many years.	You are open to living somewhere else. You are willing to move.

Default can be costly.	The costs of default don't bother you.
Benefit of home outweighs cash drain.	Don't want to waste cash.
You need a high credit rating.	Don't need to access new credit for a few years.

Okay, say you bought your home for $600,000 and your mortgage balance is $500,000, but the property value is now only $300,000. If you sold your house today, you would have to pay $200,000 plus costs, and you will lose all of the money you put into the house. What are the chances that your local property values will rise as fast as they fell? Or did you overpay when you bought your home at the very top of the real estate bubble in 2006? No matter how you look at it, you are deep underwater. A strategic default looks very attractive.

2. Strategic Defaults Are Not Limited to Real Estate
The application of strategically defaulting has focused on real estate. However, many people are strategically defaulting on credit cards and business loans. The principles of cost versus reward are the same.

One question you need to consider is that if you choose to default on one account, such as a credit card, how many other assets do you have that you may need to protect? If you default on a credit card, the card issuer will send your account to a collections agency. You can ignore them. But the collection agency may then take you to court. You cannot ignore the court. The court can levy a judgment against you and force you to pay at least some portion of the debt.

3. Strategic Defaults Are Always a Decision to Protect Cash Flow, Savings, and Wealth

The primary reasons any debtor, whether a business, individual, or even a government decides not to pay a debt are because of cash flow and savings. As in the example above, there comes a tipping point at which the cash savings from a strategic default outweighs the social, legal, and cash costs.

4. The Time Value of Asset Appreciation/Depreciation and Earnings Growth/Decline Is a Key Factor of Strategic Default

The world is recovering from a huge liquidity bubble that drove asset prices beyond reasonable levels. In fact, during the past ten years the rise in asset valuations was simply a measure of investors' demands for securities connected to assets and the ability of investment banks to sell "securitized instruments" to meet that demand. The investors wanted excellent cash returns and the investment banks were more than happy to deliver. In order to deliver, any and all assets were used as a security to sell investors on securitized instruments. Investors were led to believe there was little or no risk. Home mortgages, credit card receivables, auto loans, and student loans were all bundled into securitized investments.

It doesn't take an advanced degree in economics to understand that assets that were overpriced during the bubble will take years to recover their value, if they ever do. Unemployment numbers continue to rise. In the current economic climate, the only businesses making money are ones that are slashing jobs, exporting services and labor to other countries, or are receiving some form of government subsidy or guarantee. Globally, many governments are deep in debt and the outlook is that an economic recovery will be a long and painful process. We have already seen, for example, riots in the streets of Greece due to severe government cutbacks spurred by the demands of the International Monetary Fund (IMF).

Given these basic factors, why should any individual or business invest its cash into an overvalued asset that has little chance of regaining its original value?

5. An Asset Can Now Be Purchased for a Fraction of the Cost of the Same Asset at its Peak Value

This can be summed up from the numerous clients I have talked with as follows: "Why should we continue to pay the mortgage when we can rent the same property down the street for half the cost?"

It is painful to sit on the front porch of the dream home you bought in 2006 for $500,000, and as the sun sets and you sip your white wine you look across the street and see your neighbor's house, which is just as nice as yours, on the market for $200,000. You cannot help but feel like a chump. You are paying $3,000 a month on your mortgage over 30 years. If you moved across the street to your neighbor's house, you would pay only $1,500 a month! Or, if you don't mind paying $3,000 a month, you could trade up to a house bigger than yours with a pool and solarium and three-car garage in a nicer neighborhood closer to the beach.

And here's the flip side that will really make your blood boil. If you are paying $3,000 a month to your mortgage servicer, where does that cash go? Chances are, the lender is re-investing it. Your lender can take your mortgage payment and (to oversimplify a bit) can buy your neighbor's house for $1,500 a month and then with the extra $1,500 buy the house next door to you! So while you are being a loyal customer and honoring your contract with your lender, your lender is free to take your cash and make investments that allow it to make even more cash. Your lender has the big lever and you have a toothpick.

And if your lender is a member of the Mortgage Bankers Association, they already know all about strategic default, because the MBA has done it.

6. Strategic Defaults Are a Business Decision to Break a Contract, Not a Moral Decision

First and foremost, there is not one single lender who loans money based on moral decisions. Simply review the loan agreement. It contains a wide range of conditions and obligations regarding the repayment of the loan. And when it comes to a default in a loan, the written agreements contain a wide range of options to collect. These options include:

- Seizing and/or foreclosing on an asset.
- The option to sue the debtor personally and seize the debtor's assets or garnish wages.
- The option to make negative reports on the debtor's credit.

There is no moral punishment for not paying the debt. The lender will not stand over you and say, "You have committed wrong by not paying me and you shall now suffer eternal damnation." No, the lender goes to court, not to a house of worship or spiritual leader.

Make no mistake: your lender is in business to make money. And business is business, as they say. It's not personal and it's not based on abstract morality.

7. Debt Is Similar to the Physics Principle of Matter and Energy

There is a principle in physics that matter and energy can neither be created nor destroyed; they can only be rearranged. Debt follows the same lines. Once debt is created it cannot be destroyed unless it is restructured and resolved. This means that a strategic default does not eliminate debt unless you restructure and resolve it. Debt will follow you until it is restructured and resolved. A lender has a certain period of time to collect debt, not unlike a statute of limitations. In certain states a lender has up to 20 years. With certain limitations, a lender or creditor can seek to collect on its debt anytime before a statute of limitations expires.

8. A Strategic Default Is Measured in Years, Not Days or Months

Any decision to walk away from debt begins a long process. The process can last years. It can take a lender or creditor a year or more to foreclose on a property. It can take you three to four years to repair your credit. It can take a year or more to pay back a debt.

It can take a lender or creditor a year or more to win a court action to collect money. You can live in your property, payment free, for a year or more before a lender can successfully foreclose. It can take a year or more before you regain your personal and financial confidence. A lender or creditor can spend a year or more trying to collect a debt through a long process involving letters, phone calls, and/or legal action.

9. States and the Federal Government Have Laws That Protect You from Deficiency and Forgiven Debt

On December 27, 2007, President Bush signed the Mortgage Forgiveness Debt Relief Act of 2007 into law.[xi]

This law established a three-year moratorium (now extended to December 2012 by the Emergency Economic Stabilization Act of 2008) that prevents any debt forgiven by a lender from being counted as income by the IRS. Basically, if a homeowner negotiates a short sale or any other type of debt forgiveness with a lender, the homeowner will not be liable for any taxes on the forgiven debt. This applies to primary residences not second homes or investment properties.

For example, if a homeowner in foreclosure gets a bank to agree to take $400,000 for an original loan amount of $500,000, then the homeowner will not have to pay any taxes on the forgiven $100,000 ($500,000 minus the $400,000). This is a federal law, so your state taxation department may not apply the same rules.

State laws regulate the actions that creditors can take when trying to collect on a secured loan. In some cases, states prohibit the creditor from seeking more than the collateral used to secure the loan. This is called "non-recourse" or "anti-deficiency," meaning that a creditor cannot hold the borrower personally liable for more than the value of the property at the time of sale. Generally, in a non-recourse state, if a lender cannot recoup its loan from the sale or seizure of the asset used for collateral, then the relevant state law will limit the lenders ability to collect from the borrower.

In a non-recourse state, if you default on your home loan, the bank can only foreclose on the home. If the sale proceeds are not enough to repay the loan, the bank cannot take further action or the bank is limited on what it can collect. For example, in a non-recourse jurisdiction such as California, if a borrower owes a lender a $100,000 deficiency after the completion of a short sale or a foreclosure sale, under most circumstances the lender cannot get the money from the borrower. Each state implements "non-recourse" or "anti-deficiency" laws differently.

As of this writing, the following states have some form of non-recourse or anti-deficiency law:

Alaska, Arizona, California, Connecticut, Iowa, North Carolina, North Dakota, Minnesota, Montana, Oregon, and Washington.

There are also "one-action" states, which means that lenders are only permitted a single legal action to collect mortgage debt. Individual state laws vary. In New York, for example, a lender must choose between the actions of suing to collect the debt or foreclosing on the property. The following states have some type of one-action statute:

California, Idaho, Montana, Nevada, New York, and Utah.

In a recourse jurisdiction such as Ohio, if a borrower owes a lender a $100,000 deficiency after a short sale or a foreclosure sale, the lender can chase the borrower for the difference, i.e., get a personal judgment against a borrower. However, most recourse states have very strict rules governing the process of obtaining deficiency judgments. If a lender does not follow the rules in a recourse state, then it may not be able to obtain a deficiency judgment.

As of this writing, these are the recourse states:

Alabama, Arkansas, Colorado, Delaware, District of Columbia (D.C.), Florida, Georgia, Hawaii, Illinois, Idaho, Indiana, Kansas, Kentucky, Louisiana, Maine, Maryland, Massachusetts, Michigan, Mississippi, Missouri, Ohio, Nebraska, Nevada, New Hampshire, New Jersey, New Mexico, New York, Oklahoma, Pennsylvania, Puerto Rico, Rhode

Island, South Carolina, Tennessee, Texas, Utah, Vermont, Virginia, West Virginia, Wisconsin, and Wyoming.

State laws vary. If you are considering a strategic default, consult your state law regarding the creditor's rights to collect.

10. Strategic Default Is a Growing Phenomenon, and the Battle Lines Are Being Drawn

If you think strategic default is not on the mind of average people, big banks, and the government, think again. CBS's *60 Minutes*, *The Wall Street Journal*, Fox News, Glenn Beck, Bloomberg, ABC News, MSNBC, *Financial Times, The Los Angeles Times, BusinessWeek*, Freddie Mac, newspapers, local newspapers, university professors, online (just type in the Google search "strategic default") and governments officials are all talking about and writing about strategic default.

You may ask, "Why all the hype now, especially since governments, nations, investors and businesses have been strategically defaulting for thousands of years?" The reason is that the consumer, the so-called engine of economic growth, is now getting into the act. The consumer has consumed to capacity and does not want to carry all of the dead weight. The consumer has decided to push the losses of inflated assets onto the back of government and business. This is where the battle lines have been drawn. Government and business want consumers to pay their debt under any circumstance no matter how financially devastating.

Consumers are starting to act like business people and leaving emotion aside. This is an issue that strikes at the fabric of society. It is the idea that all debt (with interest, fees, and penalties) is expected to be and must be paid in full by consumers. Expect to see a struggle coming from both sides. As this is a fight about who bears the burden of the negative equity produced by our collective excess spending, excess lending, and excess consumption.

11. Every Strategic Default Is Unique to the Circumstances of the Individual and/or Businesses

Only you can decide when you have reached the tipping point and if it is in the best interests of you, your family, or your business, to strategically default. For some, a decision to strategically default is a piece of cake. There are no moral or ethical qualms. For others it can be an agonizing decision involving a wide range of emotions. There may be feelings of anxiety, fear, hopelessness, and anger. Especially when lenders stonewall on loan modifications and when the government bails out banks and big business.

The future may seem uncertain, yet after carefully considering a strategic default and implementing a strategic default, there should be a feeling of relief and a sense of empowerment. This arises from your personal decision to take total control your financial future.

5. Cost, Benefit, and Risk

A strategic default is a decision that is based on what is best for you, your family, or your business. In order to make the best decision you should carefully calculate the costs and benefits of your action.

This is not to say that morality and emotional concerns are not a factor. It is. There are moral, emotional, and social issues that arise when making a decision to stop making loan payments when the money is available. These moral and social issues intersect with an individual's "rational" decision to stop losing money. Our society generally places a strong taboo against breaking an agreement. We use time-honored expressions such as "a man's word is his bond" and "a deal's a deal."

Fear also plays a significant role in the decision to strategically default. There is a real fear that any decision to stop making loan payments could lead to future financial ruin. What you may not understand is that a lender or creditor cannot take your house the moment you stop making payments. There is a long legal process that must occur before you can lose your home. During that time you can defend yourself, save money, or make plans to stay or move. The same holds true for any attempts to collect on any type of debt. The only weapon against fear is knowledge.

One may feel shame, guilt, hopelessness, and anger. These are the emotions associated with the perception that you may be a financial failure or that you have broken a promise. These emotions arise from lenders failure to help homeowners. It also arises from the government's insistence to bailout banks with taxpayer monies. Yet, keep in mind that the some of the smartest and wealthiest individuals also experienced financial failure.

In an excellent analysis of this phenomenon, University of Arizona law professor Brent T. White writes of the moral and social reasons why property owners do not strategically default even though it's in their best interest to do so.[xii] He also writes that "many strategic defaulters feel great anxiety about their financial situation, are overwhelmed by a sense of hopelessness, and are angry that their lenders and the government refuse to help." Yet, there is one statement by Professor White that is a theme for this book: "Strategic default might not only be a viable option, but also the wisest financial decision."

In the end, it boils down to "doing the math" and asking yourself, "How is my current course of action working for me and my loved ones?"

Respect the Lender's or Creditor's Perspective

A lender or creditor has only one goal in mind: to collect every penny of the outstanding debt, including interest, fees, late fees, legal fees, and every imaginable cost. The lender's representatives are trained to collect as much as possible for as long as possible. So don't be fooled. Any promise by a lender's representative that takes money out of their pocket and keeps it in yours is too good to be true. A lender will not give anything away unless you demand it. Do not assume a lender is looking out for your best interests. The lender is responsible only to the management of the business and/or to its shareholders.

Follow a Business Decision Approach

Every business decision is based on two eternally intertwined yet opposing forces: cost and benefit. In business there can be no benefit without cost, but the trick is to always decide on the course of action that will produce the greatest benefit at the lowest cost. When preparing your strategic default, you should do the same.

There is one additional factor. If every business calculation were a simple comparison of cost and benefit, we would all be millionaires.

Risk is the final element that makes the difference after all it's not called "strategic default" for nothing. Even the most carefully calibrated strategy is subject to outside or unpredictable forces. Your house may be flooded in a once-every-century storm. The real estate market may tumble. Your family may suffer from a tragedy. The laws may change. A crack dealer may move in next door. Your city sewer system may break down sending sewage into your basement and your insurance company may refuse to pay. You name it, and it could happen.

What you need to do is evaluate the risks, rewards, and benefits of your plan. The best way to do this is to write them down.

Time Line

The first step is to develop a time line of what is going to happen when you default. You need to be able to plan your future and stay in control of the process. Below is a generic time line for a home mortgage default. Conditions and events will vary according to federal law, your state laws and your lender's choices.

TIME	ACTION
1 month	You stop paying your mortgage.
2 months	Your lender assesses late fees and tries to contact you. At the end of 60 days your lender will send you a demand letter.
3-5 months	Your lender refers your loan to its foreclosure department. They hire a local attorney to initiate foreclosure. They may file notice with the local court.
7-14 months	Your house is sold at a foreclosure auction. If you have not moved out, you are still the legal tenant. The new owner must now initiate eviction proceedings. Depending on state laws and your family circumstances, you may be able to live in the house several more months.
Post-foreclosure	Depending on state law regulating lender recourse, your lender will attempt to recoup the deficit owed from the property sale. If you live in a recourse state, your lender may try to sue you for the deficit and all costs.
Seven years	The foreclosure remains on your credit history for seven years from the date of the first public filing (not the date of the actual sale).

Now you need to make a cost vs. benefit chart. This will enable you to take an objective look at your plan. Every plan is different, but yours may look like this.

COST	BENEFIT
Loss of house in foreclosure.	Rent another house for half the cost.
Social stigma of foreclosure.	Attitudes are changing. My neighbor did it.
Negative credit report.	Don't expect to get any new lines of credit.
Stress of default process.	Removal of the risk of forced default if you become ill or cannot pay your old, inflated mortgage.
Dipping into savings or throwing cash away.	Protection of savings, cash put to better use, invest the extra money.

Next you should create a form listing your monthly expenses and available cash for both scenarios—staying on course or defaulting. It is assumed that your income will remain the same. The point of the chart is to identify the free cash created by the strategic default, and then to identify an objective for the cash. Remember that one option that may be closed to you for a few years is getting another mortgage to buy another house. A prospective lender will almost certainly cite your credit history as a reason to decline your loan application.

	LIVING EXPENSE	FREE CASH
Pay mortgage	$3,000	$500
Strategic default	$1,500	$2,000

Questions to Consider When Deciding to Strategically Default

- What is the impact of the debt on cash flow?
- What is the impact of the debt on cash savings, retirement funds, IRA, or any other investment? Do you have to "dip" into your savings to pay your bills?
- When will a good credit score be important to you? Do you need more credit? Do you need to do anything requiring a good credit score? Will poor credit negatively affect your business?
- Do you understand all of the risks of strategic default?
- What are your short- and long-term financial goals? Are you near retirement?
- Can you get a better return if your money is put to a better use? Will the "better return" be greater than the financial cost of strategically defaulting?
- Do you know the time line from when you decide to stop paying a lender until a lender can successfully recover a debt? Did you know it can take a lender months or years to collect depending on the circumstances?
- Are you prepared for the creditor harassment? Phone calls, letters, and legal threats? Are you prepared to fight back against this? Did you explore all of your available options – short sale, loan modification, refinance, principle reduction, or deed-in-lieu of foreclosure?
- Did you know that any time a lender agrees to change any loan term, in any manner; it will negatively affect your credit?
- Did you know that a drop in your credit score may impact existing credit cards and/or loans? For example, you could see a rise in credit card interest rates or a

reduction in credit card limits or home equity lines once you decided to strategically default.

- Do you know how to legally protect your assets, savings, and cash flow from creditors?
- Are you prepared to aggressively defend against debt collection efforts and actions? Did you know that you have the right to challenge a creditor's right to collect a debt? For example, does the creditor have the proper paperwork establishing the debt?

6. Consequences of Strategic Default

If there were no consequences to walking away from a debt, everyone would do it. But you have signed a contract and your creditor has significant rights. Let's review what can happen when you strategically default. Then you can decide for yourself if it's worth it.

Lawsuit

If the borrower defaults on a valid loan agreement, a lender can sue a borrower for any unpaid amounts on a loan. If a lender obtains a judgment after starting a proper legal action for the unpaid amount, the lender or creditor may have the right to garnish wages, place a lien on a bank account or property. A personal judgment can last up to 20 years in certain states.

Tax liability

If a lender agrees to forgive any unpaid loan amount, then under certain circumstances the portion of the debt that is forgiven may be considered taxable income.

Seizing collateral

A lender has the right to seize an asset that is secured by the debt after commencing a proper legal action. For example, a lender can force the sale of a property to satisfy an unpaid mortgage debt (foreclosure). A lender can seize business equipment or any other property that is pledge as collateral to secure the debt if it remains unpaid.

Credit score impact

A credit score will be severely impaired for a certain period of time, thereby reducing the ability to obtain credit or a loan. It negatively affects an individual's or business's credit profile. The primary credit reporting agencies (Equifax, Experian, and Trans Union) regularly report payment information. These companies also report defaults, foreclosures, short sales, debt settlements, judgments, and other adverse financial information. The main credit reporting agency for businesses, Dun & Bradstreet, also reports negative payment information.

Government actions

In the case of a government loan, such as an SBA loan, the SBA can seize income tax refunds, garnish a portion of government checks, seize money from bank accounts, and place a lien on any asset. The government does not need to start a legal action to do this.

Keeping cash in a bank account with the same lender to whom you owe a debt

Banks are exercising their right to take funds from a checking or savings account to pay off a defaulted loan, mortgage or credit card that originated from the same bank. The bank simply takes the money with no notice. Once it happens, the bank will tell you that you agreed to let that happen when you opened the account. So if you are defaulting on a Chase credit card then you should not have your checking or savings account with Chase. If you are defaulting on your Bank of America mortgage then you should not have your checking or savings account with Bank of America. If you are a guarantor for any type of loan then make sure you do not have a savings or checking account at the same bank.

Continued liability for debts or obligations associated with the property

You are still responsible for other debts and obligations associated with a property when a decision is made to strategically default. For example, many property owners have second mortgages or home equity lines of credits (HELOC). There are payments due for local real estate taxes, school taxes, utilities, water bills, insurance, homeowner association dues, and other costs associated with carrying the property. These debts or obligations do not disappear after a strategic default. A lender can sue for personal judgment on a second mortgage or HELOC since there is little chance the lender will be paid at a foreclosure sale, short sale, or deed-in-lieu. The local government taxing authority may seek to collect on any outstanding real estate tax or water bill. Keep in mind strategic default is all encompassing. If a bill is not paid it can be become a debt obligation that follows you. All debts must be dealt with so do not ignore the smaller obligations.

Mortgage loan risks

Here are some consequences that are specific to mortgage loan defaults:

- A lender can start a foreclosure action to force the sale of a property.

- A lender has the right to obtain a deficiency judgment. A deficiency judgment is a judgment lien against a borrower for the difference between what is collected at a foreclosure sale and what is owed to the bank. For example, if a lender sells a property for $400,000 at a foreclosure action and the lender was owed $450,000, the borrower can be liable to the lender for the $50,000 difference. The $50,000 owed to the lender can become a deficiency judgment.

- Deficiency judgments are transferable. Currently, there are investors and real estate professionals purchasing deficiency judgments from lenders at substantial discounts, sometimes at 10 cents on the dollar or less. Once purchased, these new owners of the deficiency debt may seek to recover 40 to 50 cents on the dollar from the debtor and make a tidy profit.

- A mortgage lender has the right to seek a court-appointed receiver to collect rents or income during a foreclosure action. The loan documents may give a lender the right to seek the appointment of a receiver to collect rents or income. In fact, there may be language contained in the loan documents giving the lender an assignment of leases and rents. Furthermore, loan documents can give a lender a "security interest" in the property contained inside a residential and commercial property and contained in a business. While it appears many lenders do not seek the appointment of a receiver for one to four family properties, it can change if lenders face growing losses. It is common to seek the appointment of a receiver for commercial property foreclosures.

- In the case of a mortgage loan, a lender can sue for a personal judgment instead of foreclosing. A mortgage lender has the right to forgo a foreclosure lawsuit and instead sue a borrower personally for the loan. Lenders holding second mortgage liens on a property are beginning to sue borrowers personally.

- There may be a violation of state or federal rent skimming laws. Rent skimming means taking the money received from a rent and not applying the funds towards mortgage payments. For example, California has a law against rent skimming. Among other aspects of the law, it is unlawful to collect rent and not pay the mortgage during the first year after the property was purchased.

Fannie Mae Regulations

On June 23, 2010, Fannie Mae, the nation's second-largest mortgage company, issued a press release announcing a new rule to punish strategic defaulters. The key parts to the policy are as follows:

1. If a borrower walks away and a.) has the capacity to pay, or b.) does not complete a work out in good faith (workouts are defined as loan modifications, short sales, and deed-in-lieu), then the borrower will be ineligible for any new Fannie Mae-backed mortgage loan for a period of seven years from the date of foreclosure.

2. Fannie Mae will actively take legal action to recoup outstanding mortgage debt from borrowers who strategically default in jurisdictions that allow for deficiency judgments. Fannie Mae will be instructing servicers and lenders to essentially provide information on delinquent loans facing foreclosure and ask these same servicers and lenders to put forth recommendations for cases that warrant deficiency judgments.

This has the potential to create serious issues if you hope to secure a Fannie Mae-backed mortgage after a strategic default.

7. Know the Legal Landscape

Your creditors have access to high-powered legal services. They're pros and they know the law. When you embark on a strategic default, your creditor will respond with a well-choreographed set of actions that has probably produced favorable results for them in the past.

But the law can also protect you. Tactics that may be used by aggressive collections agencies or lawyers may include suggestions of consequences that may not be accurate. If your house is sold at foreclosure, for example, you will almost certainly receive a phone call from the new owner's lawyer telling you to move out immediately. You may not have to, and if you know your state's eviction laws and federal laws you will be able to deal from a position of strength.

Here are some questions that you need to be able to answer.

- Are you prepared for the creditor harassment? Phone calls, letters, and possible legal threats? Are you prepared to fight back against this? Refer to the **Fair Debt Collections Practices Act**[xiii] to learn more about federal debt collection rules and regulations. There are other laws that protect you and govern the collection of debt.

- Did you explore all of your available options – short sale, loan modification, refinance, principle reduction, or deed-in-lieu of foreclosure? Did you ask your lender for a principle reduction?

- Did you speak with a professional such as an attorney, or did you go to the court house if you were unsure of what you were doing? Did you contact a non-profit agency specializing in loan default or foreclosure assistance?

- Did you respond to all court papers in time and in writing? Did you respond to all demand letters within the 30-day period and in writing? Did you ask the lender or creditor to provide every agreement or promise made in writing? Did you receive proper written notices from the lender or creditor before they took any action?

- Did you know that a drop in your credit score may impact existing credit cards and/or loans? For example, you could see a rise in credit card interest rates or a reduction in credit card limits or home equity lines once you decided to strategically default. Check out the recently enacted Credit Card Accountability, Responsibility, and Disclosure Act of 2009[xiv] (the CARD Act). The Act offers protection against "universal default," the practice of raising interest rates on customers if they are late paying an unrelated bill, such as a car loan or a utility bill, which is now prohibited for existing balances. But new purchases or cash advances can be charged a higher rate.

- Do you know how to legally protect your assets, savings, and cash flow from creditors? Are you prepared to do so?

- Did you know that each state and the federal government are creating laws to protect homeowners?

- Did you know that under federal law, as the homeowner you have the right to stay in your home for at least 90 days after a foreclosure sale?

- Did you know that under federal law, as the homeowner you have the right to stay in your home for at least 90 days after a foreclosure sale?

- Did you know that you can challenge the creditor's ability to collect the debt? Did you know that you have the legal right to ask a lender for all of the documents proving the existence and ownership of the debt at any time before or during a lawsuit to collect the debt? Did you know that if a creditor or lender is unable to legally prove the validity of a debt then the debt may not be able to collect the debt?

8. The Process

It's time to get organized! Here's a guide to what you need to do to initiate and survive a strategic default.

1. Prepare an Action Plan

You need to decide your plan of attack. Your action plan should ask the following questions:

a. What is your number #1 goal?
b. What else do you seek to achieve?
c. What steps are you going to take?
d. How can you reduce expenses and increase cash?
e. What do you want to do with the cash, how will you protect your savings?
f. What are your general notes on your strategy for success?

2. Prepare an Income, Expense, Available Cash, Assets, and Liabilities worksheet

You need to be aware of all current income, all current expenses, all savings, and everything you own. Strategic Default is a business decision so you must treat it as such. This will give you a snap shot of your current financial picture. Your goal is to put your money to its best use and to protect everything you own now and in the future.

3. Keep All of Your Records and Keep Track of All Calls

It is important to keep all of your records. Most people get into a habit of throwing away letters. Don't do it. Find some time to purchase a file storage box. Make sure that everything that involves your debt is placed into that box. Make sure to keep track of phone calls. This includes getting the name, ID number, and the purpose of the call. If a lender calls you too frequently or harasses you at work, you can use a cease-and-desist letter to stop the calls. Tactics that collection agencies and lenders use are governed by the federal Fair Debt Collection Practices Act and state debt collection laws.

A cease-and-desist letter is an effective tool to stop creditor calls. Keep in mind the debt still remains open so it will be your responsibility to contact the original creditor to resolve it.

You can use the sample cease-and-desist letter in Appendix A.

4. Never Assume the Collection of the Debt Is Valid

While in most cases, a borrower owes the money to the lender, it is also true that the amount owed may not be correct. Always request a lender or creditor to establish the validity of the debt in writing.

If the debt is being collected by the original lender, ask the lender for a copy of any signed agreement, a transcript of all applied and missed payments, charges, and escrows, and proof that the original lender or new creditor actually owns the debt. A RESPA sample request letter template can be found on the U.S. Department of Housing and Urban Development (HUD) website.[xv] A RESPA request letter is used to get information about your mortgage.

You can use the sample RESPA request letter in Appendix B.

If the debt has been turned over to an outside debt collection agency, you need to send a debt validation letter.

This requires the collection agency to prove that they have the right to collect the debt. If they cannot prove it they cannot collect it.

You can use the sample Debt Validation Letter in Appendix C.

In this letter you exert your rights under the Fair Debt Collection Practices Act, 15 USC 1692g Sec. 809 (b). This section of the FDCPA stipulates that you may dispute the collector's claim and that you are asking for verification of their claim against you. Send a certified letter asking for the following:

- The amount of the debt.
- The name of the creditor to whom the money is owed.
- The account number.
- How did the collector determine the amount owed.
- Copies of the original creditor credit contract showing your signature.
- Proof that the statute of limitations has not lapsed for the account in question.
- Proof that the collector is licensed to collect in your state.

State that you will sue the collection agency if they file a negative credit report, or if you find any negative information on your credit as a result of their actions. This relates to provisions of the Fair Credit Reporting Act and the Fair Debt Collection Practices Act.

Inform the collector that they have 30 days to provide you with the information requested. Once they send you proof of the debt they are trying to collect, you require an additional 30 days to verify their information. During this period all phone calls, letters etc. shall cease and desist or you will file harassment charges.

5. Don't Be Credit Sensitive

A strategic default will appear on your credit history as a foreclosure (because that's what your lender will have to do: foreclose on your house and sell it at auction). Your credit score will be negatively affected for seven years.

According to the Fair Isaac Corp. (FICO), for mortgage-related problems the *average* points lost on a FICO score are as follows:

- 30 days late: 40 to 110 points.
- 90 days late: 70 to 135 points.
- Foreclosure, short sale or deed-in-lieu: 85 to 160.
- Bankruptcy: 130 to 240.

If your credit score were 650, a strategic default on a home mortgage would knock it down to 550 or below. Depending upon your FICO score and your ability to create positive credit items after your default, you will have to wait two to five years before a mortgage loan originator will offer you a reasonable interest rate on a home loan. You may also have difficulty getting a car loan or a new credit card. The best thing to do is to prepare in advance by making sure that you don't need to buy a car or get a new credit card for a few years, and keep up with your payments on the other credit accounts for which you owe monthly payments.

6. Respect Your Lender's Debt Collection Procedures

For all types of secured and unsecured debt, federal and state laws regulate the methods governing how and when debt collectors can contact you, what they can say, and what legal recourse they have. The Federal Trade Commission (FTC) enforces the Fair Debt Collection Practices Act (FDCPA), which prohibits debt collectors from using abusive, unfair, or deceptive practices to collect from you. The Act covers most personal debts including credit cards, auto loans, mortgages, and medical bills. Debt collectors are defined as those individuals or companies who collect debts owed to others. They may be debt collection agencies, lawyers, or companies that buy debt and then attempt to collect.

Under FDCPA, a debt collector may NOT:

- Contact you before eight o'clock in the morning or after nine o'clock at night.
- Contact you at work if they're told (orally or in writing) that you're not allowed to get calls there.
- Contact third parties (other than your attorney) except for one contact to obtain your address, your home phone number, and where you work. Collectors usually are prohibited from contacting third parties more than once.
- Harass, oppress, or abuse you or any third parties they contact.
- Lie when they are trying to collect a debt.
- Say that you will be arrested if you don't pay your debt.
- Give false credit information about you to anyone, including a credit reporting company.
- Attempt to collect any interest, fee, or other charge on top of the amount you owe unless the contract that created your debt, or your state law, allows the charge.
- Garnish most federal benefits such as Social Security payments.

For a complete list of what debt collectors can and cannot do, go to the Federal Trade Commission Debt Collection FAQs page at:
http://www.ftc.gov/bcp/edu/pubs/consumer/credit/cre18.shtm

The federal Fair Debt Collection Practices Act does not apply to original creditors, like a mortgage lender or credit card company. However, most state laws reflect the FDCP law in regard to original creditors. For example, California's Rosenthal Fair Debt Collection Practices Act (Civil Code Section 1788-1788.3)[xvi] covers both original creditors and debt collection agencies. For more information, consult your state law.

Therefore, if you need to assert your legal rights against the collection practices of your original mortgage lender, credit card company, or medical services provider, you will need to cite state law, not the federal FDCPA.

7. Protect and Preserve Your Cash, Savings, and Assets

A part of your strategic default plan should include consideration of asset protection. For most debts, your creditor will have to file suit in court in order to force you to relinquish any asset. However, in the case of mortgage default, you need to prepare for a **deficiency debt**.

A deficiency debt is the difference between the outstanding balance of the mortgage note, plus costs and attorneys' fees, and the received income of the property foreclosed. For example, let's say your foreclosed property sells at auction for $250,000. Your mortgage balance is $325,000 and your lender claims another $5,000 in foreclosure costs and fees. That's a total of $330,000 against the sale income of $250,000. A deficiency debt can lead to a deficiency judgment. Your lender may start a lawsuit to obtain a deficiency judgment against you for $80,000, and this can come out of your pocket. A deficiency judgment can obliterate the reason why it was advantageous for you to default: it represents about two years' worth of future mortgage payments.

Check your state law. In Florida, for example, a cash shortfall at the mortgage foreclosure sale does not automatically lead to a deficiency judgment. To obtain a deficiency judgment against you, after the foreclosure sale the lender must file a court motion for a deficiency. The court then holds an evidentiary hearing on the lender's request for deficiency liability. At the evidentiary hearing the mortgage lender must prove that the property's value on the sale date was less than the note balance. You have the opportunity to demonstrate that the value of the house was greater than the amount of the note, and to make your case you can introduce independent appraisals or government tax assessments.

Deficiency judgments increase during real estate downturns, especially from holders of second mortgages. Your best bet is to hire a qualified attorney and prove the property had a higher value, delay the motion, or negotiate a settlement. If you have $80,000 at stake, a few thousand dollars for a good lawyer is worth it.

There may be **tax issues** as well. If your lender forgives part of your debt, such as in a short sale, you may receive a 1099 form stating that the deficiency is personal income. But the federal Mortgage Debt Relief Act of 2007 generally allows taxpayers to exclude income from the discharge of debt on their *principal residence*. Debt reduced through mortgage restructuring, as well as mortgage debt forgiven in connection with a foreclosure, qualifies for the relief. This provision applies to debt forgiven in calendar years 2007 through 2012. The IRS states that "Up to $2 million of forgiven debt is eligible for this exclusion ($1 million if married filing separately). The exclusion does not apply if the discharge is due to services performed for the lender or any other reason not directly related to a decline in the home's value or the taxpayer's financial condition." There are other tax-related issues that may apply to you. Consult your tax specialist or a CPA for professional advice.

8. Steps To Walking Away

Here is your checklist of what you will need to do at every stage of your strategic default.

- ✓ Prepare and review your Action Plan. Determine the WHY and WHAT YOU EXPECT TO ACHIEVE.
- ✓ Prepare and review your income, expense, available cash, current assets and liabilities.
- ✓ Gather all of your loan documents.
- ✓ Prepare a log to keep track of all communications with the lender or creditor.
- ✓ Apply the Strategic Default principles and understand the risks.
- ✓ Hire the necessary professionals: attorney, accountant or tax specialist, and real estate brokers.
- ✓ Become familiar with federal and state rules regarding foreclosure actions. Each state has rules regarding foreclosure. Keep in mind a lender can sell the debt to a third party collector.
- ✓ Prepare a time line.
- ✓ Send a RESPA Request Letter (form) by certified mail to the lender and request your loan documents, a financial transcript of all payments, charges, fees, legal fees, escrows, proof of proper ownership of debt.
- ✓ Prepare to successfully negotiate a loan modification, principle reduction, short sale, deed-in-lieu. If a foreclosure action begins make sure your respond, in writing. Get a lawyer or go to the court if you are not comfortable representing yourself. Always fight back.

- ✓ Plan to move out of the property, or stay in the property after the foreclosure auction and negotiate the eviction notice. There may be state laws or federal laws that allow you to stay.
- ✓ Prepare for deficiency action.

9. Other Types of Strategic Default

Walking Away from a Credit Card

Here is your checklist of what you will need to do at every stage of your credit card default.

- ✓ Prepare and review your Action Plan Determine the WHY and WHAT YOU EXPECT TO ACHIEVE.
- ✓ Prepare and review your income, expense, available cash, current assets and liabilities worksheet.
- ✓ Gather all of your loan documents.
- ✓ Prepare a log to keep track of all communications with the lender or creditor.
- ✓ Apply the Strategic Default principles and understand the risks.
- ✓ When you are ready, call your credit card company. State that you will default. If you want a payment plan, ask for one.
- ✓ You can negotiate a settlement with the credit card company. A credit card company may agree to take 30 cents on the dollar and give you time to pay it off. Make sure the balance of any unpaid debt is forgiven.
- ✓ Become familiar with federal and state rules regarding your rights against the actions of creditors and collection agencies. If you have not made a payment plan, they will start calling you.
- ✓ Send a demand to validate the debt by certified mail to the lender and request your loan documents, a financial

transcript of all payments, charges, fees, legal fees, escrows, and proof of proper ownership of debt.

- ✓ If your creditor files suit and you receive a court summons, do not ignore it! Get a lawyer if you are not comfortable representing yourself.
- ✓ Monitor your credit profile. You can expect to suffer a hit that will last for seven years.

Walking Away from a Business Loan

What you need to do depends in part on how your business is structured. Are you a sole proprietor? A partnership? A corporation? A non-profit? According to the type of business, your personal liability can vary greatly.

Here is your checklist of what you will need to do at every stage of your strategic default.

- ✓ Get a lawyer. Before you default on a business loan, you must determine your personal liability! Consult with your accountant and tax specialist. If you don't have them, hire them.
- ✓ Prepare and review your Action Plan Determine the WHY and WHAT YOU EXPECT TO ACHIEVE.
- ✓ Prepare and review your income, expense, available cash, current assets and liabilities worksheet.
- ✓ Gather all of your loan documents.
- ✓ Prepare a log to keep track of all communications with the lender or creditor.
- ✓ Apply the Strategic Default principles and understand the risks.
- ✓ Become familiar with federal and state rules regarding debt collection actions. Keep in mind a lender can sell the debt to a third party collector.
- ✓ Prepare a time line.

- ✓ Send a demand to validate debt letter by certified mail to the lender and request your loan documents, a financial transcript of all payments, charges, fees, legal fees, escrows, and proof of proper ownership of debt.
- ✓ Make sure to contact each person that acted as a guarantor on the debt. In many instances, a business loan involves a personal guarantee from an individual. If the business debt is not paid then the individual guarantor is responsible for everything that is owed.
- ✓ Prepare to successfully negotiate a payoff plan if this is what you want or a settlement of the debt.

10. After You Walk Away

Once you have set the wheels in motion and your house has been foreclosed or your credit card account closed, you have three main concerns: your emotional health, your personal finances, and your credit rating.

Emotional Health

How you move forward depends upon many variables: the degree of trauma (after the foreclosure were you forced to relocate to a new neighborhood?) and your attitude toward breaking a contract. Basically, you need to remind yourself that a strategic default is a tool that has been used by businesses (including the Mortgage Bankers Association and Donald Trump) when it has become clear that due to changing conditions an agreement is no longer tenable. In some ways it is like a divorce or any other reconsideration of a contract: it's no fun but at the end of the day you need to be responsible for your own well-being.

There is no one answer that fits everyone when it comes to the emotional responses to employing a strategic default. Each individual or business has a reason to do it and it all boils down to finances. In the end just remember that you are not a failure, you are a success.

Protect Your Cash and Assets

If you are like most people, your financial life post-default is governed by the same values as it was before: save for the future, don't live beyond your means, and use credit wisely. After all, your choice of a strategic default is a reflection of your ability to make tough choices about your financial future.

Like Donald Trump, you are no leaf in the wind. You are capable of shaping your destiny, redefining yourself, realigning your assets, and controlling your finances.

If you are experiencing ongoing financial stress, you may consider seeking the services of a professional debt counseling service. Be very careful. In most cases, a debt reduction or modification service will have no more leverage over your creditor(s) than you have. And you should never pay a fee up front for debt reduction (if you simply want professional advice, by all means pay for the service. Then you are done. No contracts!). If there is one rule you must follow then it is this: "Do not pay for any debt reduction, debt elimination, or loan modification service until the service is complete. Then honor the agreement to pay."

There are asset protection techniques used by the wealthy to preserve their wealth. You should also investigate these techniques and strategies. You will need to consult with a qualified attorney and accountant. Your goal should be to legally protect your assets in order to minimize any loss of wealth or cash.

Your Credit Rating

You know, or you will shortly see, that your credit score is now in the dumpster. But you were prepared for that when you chose to strategically default. And now you need to build up your score by using what credit you have wisely. There is no way to remove a lawful negative credit event from your record, but you should regularly check your credit history for inaccuracies that can hurt you. You are legally entitled to one free copy of your credit report each year. If you spot a mistake, notify the creditor by certified mail. If they cannot prove the legitimacy of the item they must remove it.

11. Frequently Asked Questions About Debt After Strategic Default

What is a Personal Debt Obligation?

A personal debt obligation is an amount of money legally owed to a lender that arises from a loan agreement. It involves a continuing obligation to make payments until the debt is paid off in full. A lender has the right to sue in order to collect any unpaid outstanding debt. A debt obligation can be secured or unsecured. A secured debt obligation involves the placement of a lien against the debtor's property, so a lender can force the sale of the property to pay off the debt. An unsecured debt obligation has no security against the debtor's property which means a lender can only sue a debtor personally to recover any monies due.

What is Debt Forgiveness?

Debt forgiveness is the partial or total forgiveness of a debt. It means you no longer owe the debt to the lender or any other party. The lender gives up its rights to collect the debt and instead "writes it off" their books. Once a lender agrees to forgive a debt, the lender will report the forgiveness to the IRS by filing a 1099 form.

What is a Deficiency Debt?

Deficiency debt also known as debt deficiency arises when collateral that is used to secure a loan cannot satisfy the total amount due on the loan. It happens most often with debt involving real estate. However, it can occur in other types of collateralized loans such as car, business, and equipment loans. When a loan goes unpaid, the lender has the right to auction off the property to pay off the debt. If the lender collects less than what is owed at the sale, the shortage is called debt deficiency.

What are the consequences of a Personal Debt Obligation?
You will continue to owe the original amount that was borrowed plus any additional interest, late fees, collections fees, penalties, and/or attorney fees that may come due. If the debt obligation remains unpaid, then the lender can go to court, sue for a money judgment, get a money judgment, and use any legally available collection tactic. Most often, after a money judgment is awarded, a lender will attempt to put a lien on a bank account or garnish wages or put a lien on the debtor's real estate. A lender can put a lien on business equipment. A debt obligation that turns into a money judgment can last for many years. In New York, a money judgment last for 20 years.

What are the consequences of Debt Forgiveness or Debt Deficiency?
Whether it is debt forgiveness or debt deficiency, the consequences are essentially the same. A lender has two general options regarding any unpaid debt:

1. The lender can forgive the debt.
2. The lender can get a court ordered money judgment to chase the borrower for the money or sell the debt to a third party.

If a lender agrees to forgive the debt, the lender will, in all likelihood, file a 1099 form for the forgiven amount. You should also remember to check your state taxing authority, since your state may consider debt forgiveness as taxable income. If the debt is secured by property, it may be possible to negotiate an exchange of the property for the full debt balance. In this case, the lender would not have a reason to file a 1099 form.

If the lender refuses to forgive the unpaid portion of a debt, then the lender will try to collect on the remaining balance. The lender can hire an attorney to sue for the remaining debt or sell the debt to a third-party. If successful, a lender will get a money judgment. There are various methods a lender can use to enforce collection of a money judgment. They can request your financial records to see if you have a job; to determine if you possess cash in the bank; or to locate your property. If the lender can find anything you own or earn, it will be seized or attached. The lender has the right to collect a fixed percentage of your wages also known as wage garnishment. By the way, the lender does not need you permission to garnish your wages. The lender simply contacts the payroll department and demands that a portion of your salary go to the lender.

When there is a debt deficiency from the sale of a property, the lender can forgive the difference or try to collect the difference. A deficiency debt becomes a new personal debt obligation unless a lender forgives the deficiency. Sometimes, a lender will demand a property owner sign another loan agreement for a deficiency debt. The IRS and some states offer tax relief to homeowners who have their debt deficiency forgiven. There is more information provided ahead about tax relief in this FAQ.

In our day and age, debt collection is big business. Technology makes it easier to find anyone and to find everything an individual earns or owns. There are third party companies purchasing personal debt obligations and/or deficiency debt from lenders. These third party companies may pay 10 to 20 cents on the dollar for the debt. Once the third party company owns your remaining debt, under most circumstances the third party has the same collection rights as the original lender.

Why does a lender issue an IRS 1099 form after Debt Forgiveness?

Debt forgiveness is considered taxable income by the IRS and by certain state and municipal taxing authorities. The IRS requires a lender to report the forgiven debt on form 1099-C, Cancellation of Debt. Individuals are required to report any forgiven debt on Form 1040. For example, let's say Mr. Jones originally borrowed $250,000 from the lender. The lender decides to forgive $150,000. The IRS believes that since you did not have to pay back the entire loan, then you ended up keeping the money. Therefore, it is income.

If I own a property with a value less than the mortgage balance, can the difference be forgiven through a short sale or a foreclosure auction? Can the difference become a deficiency debt? Will the IRS let me exclude forgiven debt and not look at it as income?

The general answer is "yes" to all of the questions. If a lender agrees to a short sale, the uncollected difference can be forgiven or it can become a personal debt obligation. If the lender forgives the difference then the amount forgiven can be considered taxable income. If the lender refuses to forgive the difference, then it becomes a personal debt obligation. This means a lender or a third party (who buys the debt obligation from the lender) has the right to legally pursue you by getting a court ordered money judgment.

If your home ends up selling at a foreclosure auction for less than what is owed, the uncollected balance is called a deficiency debt. A deficiency from a foreclosure action can be forgiven or can become a personal debt obligation. Various states have anti-deficiency statutes. These statutes prevent a lender from collecting on a deficiency. Also, the federal government enacted the Mortgage Debt Relief Act of 2007. The Mortgage Debt Relief Act of 2007 allows taxpayers to exclude income from the discharge of debt on their principal residence. Debt reduced through mortgage restructuring, as well as mortgage debt forgiven in connection with a foreclosure, may qualify for the relief. The act applies to all applicable debt forgiven between 2007 and 2012. It applies up to $2 million for joint filing and $1 million if filing separately. Make sure you read the act and get a qualified tax professional to analyze your specific situation.

The IRS has additional exceptions to the “debt forgiveness is income” rule. The most common situations when cancellation of debt income is not taxable involve qualified principal residence indebtedness, bankruptcy, insolvency, certain farm debts, non-recourse loans and other exceptions established by the IRS. You need to speak with a qualified accountant or other professional, so you understand your tax obligations.

What are Anti-Deficiency Laws?

Simply put, an anti-deficiency law prevents a lender from collecting on a deficiency debt or places limits on how much a lender can collect on a deficiency debt. A homeowner will not be held responsible for any deficiency if the property is occupied by the homeowner. Basically, the property must be the homeowner’s primary residence. The lender can only recover the property and any proceeds from a foreclosure auction sale.

Anti-deficiency laws do not prevent a lender from reporting the deficiency to the IRS. Since the lender is generally prevented from collecting the loss on a sale, the lender can report the loss to the IRS as forgiven debt.

You can contact your state attorney general or banking department to learn about any deficiency laws. You can contact a qualified attorney. There are certain states that limit a lender to only one lawsuit to collect a mortgage loan debt. So make sure you get a professional opinion about your state laws.

What happens if I settle a credit card or business loan for less than what is owed?

If negotiated properly a credit card company or lender may agree to settle a business loan or credit card debt. Normally, the unpaid balance should be forgiven. This brings up an important principle. *In order to get debt forgiveness, it must be in writing!* Just because the lender verbally tells you the debt is forgiven does not mean it is forgiven unless it is in writing. There are instances when a debtor is told the debt is forgiven only to get aggressive collection calls sometime in the future.

What is a fraudulent conveyance?

A fraudulent conveyance is a transfer of property that is made to swindle, hinder, or delay a creditor, or to put such property beyond a creditors reach. It is a serious offense. But just because an individual in debt makes a conveyance of his or her property does not mean that it is a *fraudulent* conveyance. Whether a transaction constitutes a fraudulent conveyance depends upon the existence of the intent to defraud at the time that the challenged transfer was made.

A fraudulent conveyance focuses on the intent and the value of what is transferred. If you are in doubt, consult a lawyer.

How can I determine what is best for me?

Ask yourself, "What am I trying to achieve? What are my goals?" Your answer should focus on what puts you in the best financial position in the short and long term. The focus should be on reducing your debt obligation with limited long-term negative financial impact. If debt is forgiven, then you may have a tax bill. If the debt becomes a money judgment, then wages can be garnished or certain assets can be seized. You will need a qualified team of professional advisers to assist you or you need to do a fair amount of research. Your advisers can include an accountant, attorney, and/or a consultant.

12. Strategic Default in Practice

This scenario is taken from reader questions and answers from our website www.strategicdefault.org. Please use as a general guide while recognizing that each person's situation is unique and one size does not fit all.

Michelle and Jason Johnson have two children, a 10-year old and an 18-year-old. Their 18-year-old has a partial scholarship for an out-of-state university. Michelle and Jason plan to assist with the college expenses. Their combined income is $250,000 per year. They live in California. They own two investment properties: A condo in Nevada and a townhome in Florida. They each have a credit score of 720. They have $35,000 in cash savings, a 401K, and owe $42,000 to various credit companies.

The Johnsons purchased their home for $450,000 five years ago. It is now worth $250,000. They have a first mortgage of $350,000 and a second mortgage Home Equity Line of Credit (HELOC), for $125,000. Their total monthly payment for the mortgage and HELOC is $3,500. Their monthly payment only includes real estate taxes and property insurance.

Their investment properties in Nevada and Florida are underwater. These properties are worth about 50% less than what they owe on the mortgage.

They paid $275,000 and put 15% down for the Nevada property. It is now worth $140,000. They paid $290,000 and put down 10% for the Florida property. It is now worth $150,000. They had a tenant in the Nevada property but the tenant can't pay due to job loss. They spent $1,500 in legal fees to get him out. They can't rent the Florida property because there is too much rental inventory. Even if they could, the rent they could collect will not cover the mortgage, taxes, insurance, utilities and homeowner association dues.

Michelle and Jason are current on all of their payments, but it has become a drain on their savings and lifestyle. They have been considering strategic default for some time.

The Johnsons contacted their lenders and asked for a loan modification or a principle reduction on all of their properties. Their lenders refused because they were current on all payments. Furthermore, the lender would consider the home for a loan modification, but not the investment properties.

They had contacted realtors in Nevada and Florida where the investment properties are located. They also checked out values online using Zillow.com. They learned that 30% of properties in those areas are in foreclosure.

Jason and Michelle were spending a combined $4,000 per month for their investment properties. Based on their understanding of the value of the properties it became clear the properties would never regain equity. They also understood that since they owned the investment properties for three years, it meant that most of the combined $4,000 monthly payment went to interest payments, NOT principle. One loan was an interest-only; the other loan was an option ARM (adjustable rate mortgage). They took these loans out to keep their monthly payments as low as possible. In their mind, it was obvious they were throwing away $4,000 on useless assets with no value or income.

Yet the couple is having difficulty making a decision to stop paying their mortgages. They had maintained perfect credit their whole lives. They were in fear about damage to their credit score and the repercussions. They were always on time with their bills. They had feelings of guilt if they decided to stop paying and felt a sense of moral obligation to keep to their word. At the same time they were angry and frustrated at their lenders for not agreeing to modify their loans or even engage in good faith negotiations especially since lenders received billions of dollars in bailouts when in trouble. They were fearful of the consequences of not paying their mortgage.

They decided to research their options thoroughly. Recently the couple saw a *60 Minutes* special on strategic defaults. They listened to homeowners like themselves make the decision to not pay. They were especially moved by one homeowner who basically said he was brought up to always pay his debts however it didn't make sense to destroy his family's financial future wasting money on a house with negative equity.

They finally made a decision to strategically default. First they wanted to make sure they were aware of all of the benefits and risks. They decided to follow the steps in this book.

The first course of action for Michelle and Jason was to get organized.

Step 1: Prepare an Action Plan

What do Michelle and Jason want to achieve? They want to stop the drain on their savings and they want to maintain their lifestyle. Since they have two children, they are concerned about their children's basic and educational needs.

The Johnsons plan to stop payments on all of their mortgages. This will free up an estimated $7,500 per month less non-mortgage related expenses to carry the house. They know they need to make water, utility, insurance, and tax payments even though they plan to stop mortgage payments.

They hope that the lender will modify their home mortgage. They are prepared to accept the negative equity on their home as long as the payments are lower. They really want a principle reduction of their mortgage loan.

Jason and Michelle do not want to deal with their investment properties. They understand it is a total loss. They will never recover their investments. They are familiar with some of their available options: short sale, deed-in-lieu of foreclosure, or let it go to foreclosure sale. At this point, they have no intentions of filing for bankruptcy, however circumstances may change. They will call the lender to see if the principle balance can be reduced, however they are doubtful the lender will agree.

The couple has prepared a preliminary timeline. Based on their research they have more time in Florida in comparison to California and Nevada. Their research established that it takes more time to complete a foreclosure in Florida then California and Nevada.

They consider their worst-case scenario as having to move out of their home. If their lenders are unwilling to modify their loans after the decision to strategically default, then they understand that they can eventually lose their home to a foreclosure sale. They are prepared to move and rent another place, if necessary. So they decide to prepare contingency plans for the worst-case scenario. They look at other rentals in the area that are close to their youngest child's school and close to their jobs.

The Johnsons understand that they may be personally liable for any unpaid debt owed the lender, if the sale of their properties does not fully satisfy their lender.

The couple also understands that if they strategically default, they may not be able to get a Fannie Mae or a government backed loan for some time. They recently read about the Fannie Mae rule that bars homeowners from obtaining a Fannie Mae mortgage for up to seven years if the homeowner strategically defaults. They also understand that Fannie Mae may actively seek deficiency judgments. The couple is prepared to aggressively protect their income and assets. They intend to seek a qualified attorney, accountant, and/or financial advisor in order to protect their income and assets from deficiency judgments.

The couple recognizes that their action plan is a work in progress, so they are prepared for updates and changes.

2. Prepare an Income, Expense, Available Cash, Assets, and Liabilities worksheet

The Johnsons obtain an income and expense form. They write down all the sources of their available after tax income. They list the $25,000 in savings and their 401K plan. They put down all of their expenses, including credit card payments. Even though they are upside down on their properties, the properties are still listed as an asset. They list all of their outstanding debt and financial obligations on the liability side.

They decide to add in a section for upcoming one-time expenses, such as their partial tuition and board payment for their 18-year-old child.

Now they have a basic snapshot of their financial picture.

3. Keep All of Your Records and Keep Track of All Calls

Michelle and Jason begin to gather all of their documents. They look for the original closing and loan documents from when they purchased their properties. They admit to throwing away a lot of the mail, but they still have a few pieces from their lenders. They make it a point to keep every piece of correspondence going forward. They set up a several folders for the records.

Since they are on time with their payments the only mail they receive are monthly statements. However, they set up folders for the lender collection letters and possible legal notices.

They keep a sample cease-and desist-letter handy, just in case they receive aggressive collection calls.

4. Never Assume the Collection of the Debt Is Valid

The idea of challenging the validity of their debt never crossed Michelle and Jason mind. They acknowledge that they definitely owe the money. They do not believe they were victims of predatory or unscrupulous lending methods. However, what do they have to lose? If the lender made a mistake or error during the loan origination process, perhaps they can use it as leverage to negotiate. Furthermore, they did notice some escrow balances on their monthly mortgage statement. They would like more clarity.

They decide to put together a general RESPA request letter seeking information about the loan documents and the application of their monthly payments against their mortgage balance.

This brought up the issue of their credit cards. They consider a strategic default on their credit cards. They decided to hold off since they have low interest rates and the balances are less than fifty percent of the available credit. The lenders have not unilaterally raised the interest rate, charges unwarranted fees, or cut their credit. Once they stop paying their mortgages, they will keep an eye out for their credit card company's actions.

5. Don't Be Credit Sensitive

Jason and Michelle determined that they do not plan to take out any more loans or additional credit for the next three to five years. They are prepared to accept the reduction in their credit score. They also know that as long as they keep paying their other debts over time, their credit scores will start to rise when all is said and done. They will be vigilant about reviewing their credit report to make sure there is no erroneous information.

6. Respect Your Lender's Debt Collection Procedures
They have taken the time to get all of their lenders contact numbers and mailing addresses. Michelle and Jason understand that their lender will be very aggressive. The lender may attempt to contact Jason and Michelle at home, work, cell phone, or perhaps a friend or relative. Furthermore, their lenders may employ third-party collection agencies or may transfer the debt to another creditor. Most important the lenders must follow state and federal debt collection laws.

7. Protect and Preserve Your Cash, Savings, and Assets
They are most concerned about the HELOC. Since it is unlikely that the HELOC lender will see any money then the lender may sue them personally for the loan. If the lender successfully obtains a personal judgment, then Michelle and Jason's wages could be garnished or a lien can be placed against their bank account. They understand that the creditor cannot take away their 401K account.

The couple decided to consult with an accountant and an attorney regarding legal methods to protect their assets. For example, they may set up a trust for their children and fund the trust with their cash savings. They have decided to put asset protection methods in place prior to their decision to stop making payments.

They have determined that they will have an additional $7,500 per month less non-mortgage related expenses to carry the house. This may end up at $5,000 per month. They want to earn interest on this money. Essentially put it to good use. They want to get a better return on their money then the loss they will experience, if and when, the lender or creditor needs to get paid. Also, they may need this money if any debt is forgiven and they face a federal or state tax bill.

They recognize that they are under no obligation to make it easy for any creditor to collect their debt. Furthermore, they are prepared to offer a cash settlement to the HELOC lender. They may offer ten percent (10%) of the total amount due.

Jason and Michelle understand that if they do a short sale, deed-in-lieu of foreclosure or let the house go to a foreclosure sale it may lead to a deficiency judgment. It is their goal to get the lender to forgive any debt. They consult with an accountant to determine the consequences of forgiven debt under their various options.

They understand that in California, under certain circumstances their lender does not have the right to seek a personal judgment for any unpaid and uncollected balance. California is a non-recourse state. They plan to familiarize themselves with deficiency rules for Nevada and Florida, since these states are recourse states.

8. Review of Steps for Strategic Default

They take a look at the general checklist steps to walk away.

The couple decides to formulate a plan when negotiating with the lender. They have certain monthly payment and principle reductions in mind. They also know that their lenders will need proof of income, including tax returns, bank statements, and paystubs. They plan on being upfront with the lender by explaining the severity of their negative equity and the drain on their savings and monthly income. Especially with a college student.

They carefully review their costs, benefits, and risks. They review the 11 principles of strategic default to see if any principle can be best applied to their situation. For example, they realized they keep money in a checking account with the same lender holding one of their mortgages. They decide to move the money to another bank.

They carefully review the *Questions to Consider When Making A Strategic Default.*

They understand that even though the actual decision to stop making payments ca occur within days or week, the entire process can take a year or more before any final resolution.

Jason and Michelle have mentally prepared for the onslaught of collection efforts. They realize that the lender will use all available means to reach them. The lender can call their cell phone, home phone, and perhaps work phone. The lender will send letters and packages. Perhaps the lender will hire a local third party company to put notices on their door. Michelle and Jason respect all reasonable collection efforts. They will not tolerate aggressive efforts that disturb their peace.

They speak with various professionals, including an attorney and accountant to determine how the professional can best assist them. Also to determine fees for any service and when is the right time to bring the professional onto their team.

They make sure to continue to read about the ever-changing landscape of strategic defaults. They visit www.strategicdefault.org regularly for free information, strategies, news, and tips. They also visit www.debtdefense101.com regularly for free information, strategies, and news about defending against debt collection actions.

In the meantime, they are comfortable with their decision. They are confident that in the long run they will be better off.

13. Conclusion

A strategic default is a business decision to stop paying debts in order to protect cash flow, savings and wealth. It is a decision to stop putting good money into bad assets. It is a technique used by the most sophisticated investors and businesses. It has been used since the dawn of time. It involves morality, ethics, duty, security, and self-esteem.

It can be one of the most important decisions about your financial future.

It has captured the minds of people, the media, big business, and our government for one reason and one reason only: once the exclusive tool of big business, strategic default is now being used by the average person.

Even by you.

I hope this helps you understand the process more clearly. The goal is not to use a strategic default for the sake of using it. It is to shed light on a way in which many people can salvage and protect their financial future. To be free from the chains of debt that could otherwise last for decades.

To help you change your life!

Resources

You can get forms, get great resources, view videos, read articles and read real life strategic default stories, questions and answers at: www.strategicdefault.org

Please visit www.debtdefense101.com to learn offensive and defensive strategies against debt collection.

Stategicdefault.org and DebtDefense101.com are owned and operated by:

Strategic Default Infoserv, Ltd
110 Wall Street, 11th flr
New York, New York 10005

Questions can be directed to info@strategicdefault.org or controldebt@aol.com

Appendix A

Sample Cease-and-Desist Letter

Your Name
Your Address
City, State, Zip

(Sent via CERTIFIED MAIL #)

Date:

Name of Collection Agency/Law Firm
390 Main Street, #100
City Name, State, Zip

Re: File or Acct. #:_______ - (Name of Lender) -
#:____(Lender acct. #)
For: $ (amount of $$ debt collector claims you owe)

Dear Debt Collector/Debt Collector Attorney:

This letter is a written request asking you to cease and desist in your efforts to collect on the debt account as stated above. It is my personal choice to deal with the original creditor and not the collection agencies.

This is a legal notice under applicable state law and provisions of federal law, the Fair Debt Collection Practices Act (FDCPA).

If you fail to heed this notice, I will file a formal complaint against you with the Federal Trade Commission who is responsible for enforcement.

I/We have decided that we do not desire to work with a collection agency under any circumstances. I/We will contact the original creditor to resolve this matter directly, as circumstances warrant.

You are also notified that should any negative information reported to any credit bureau and subsequently placed against my/our credit reports as a result of this notice will be met with immediate action. Please respect my request.

Sincerely,

Your Name

Appendix B

Sample RESPA Request Letter

Attention Customer Service:

Subject: [Your loan number]
[Names on loan documents]
[Property and/or mailing address]

This is a "qualified written request" under Section 6 of the Real Estate Settlement Procedures Act (RESPA).

I am writing because:

- Describe the issue or the question you have and/or what action you believe the lender should take.
- Attach copies of any related written materials.
- Describe any conversations with customer service regarding the issue and to whom you spoke.
- Describe any previous steps you have taken or attempts to resolve the issue.
- List a daytime telephone number in case a customer service representative wishes to contact you.
- Request all documents in connection with the loan and proof of applied payments and escrows.

I understand that under Section 6 of RESPA you are required to acknowledge my request within 20 business days and must try to resolve the issue within 60 business days.

Sincerely,

Your Name

Appendix C

Sample Debt Validation Letter

Your Name
Your Address

VIA CERTIFIED MAIL, REGULAR MAIL & FACSIMILE
Lender/Creditor Name
Lender/Creditor Address

Re: DEMAND TO VALIDATE DEBT UNDER FEDERAL & STATE LAW Acct # XXXX-XXXX-XXXX-XXXX

To Whom It May Concern:

I am sending this letter in response to a written notice dated August 7, 2010. The notice sent by your offices claimed that I owe a certain debt to you or to a company you are affiliated with. Please be advised that this is a debt validation letter. At this time, I am not disputing the validity of the debt. I am simply requesting proof of the debt. However, I reserve the right to dispute the debt after I receive a full and complete written response to this request to validate the debt.

You are aware of the Fair Debt Collection Practices Act, in addition to my home state laws regarding debt collection practices. Under such laws, I am asserting my right to receive the following information to my requests. Be advised that when I refer to "your company", I am referring to the company that sent the notice claiming I owe a debt.

1. Who or what is the current legal owner of the debt? If your company is the owner then provide proof of the proper transfer of the debt to your company.

2. Does your company have the original paperwork that established and created the debt obligation?
3. Who or what is the name and address of the original lender of the debt? What is the date of the origination of the debt?
4. Provide a copy of all written agreements that establish the debt. Provide a copy of all written agreements allegedly signed by me as it relates to the debt.
5. Provide a written statement in which you declare that the applicable statute of limitations has not run on this debt thereby establishing you are legally entitled to collect the debt.
6. Provide an accounting of all payments made against the debt and an accounting of all fees, charges, costs, legal fees, penalties, and interest charged because of the debt.
7. Provide a verification or copy of all legal papers filed against me in an effort to collect the debt, including any judgment.
8. Provide proof that you have filed all necessary paperwork with the appropriate agencies that allow you to collect debt from me in my home state or my home city.
9. Provide each and every time your company has filed a report with any of the credit bureau as it relates to my credit report.

All collection activity must cease and desist until you have provided me with all of the requested information contained in this letter and until I have had 60 days to review the requested information. Furthermore, you shall cease and desist making any contact by telephone, email, text, facsimile, or internet phone to my home, to my place of employment, to any of my relatives, to any of my friends, and to any of my co-workers. In fact, you must cease and desist making any and all above mentioned contact to any person or entity. You may only contact me, in writing, by regular mail to the address on this letter.

Sincerely,
Your Name

Appendix D

References

---

[i] Moral and Social Constraints to Strategic Defaults on Mortgages by Luigi Guiso, Paola Spaienza, & Luigi Zingales.

[ii] *History of Visa*: See link - http://en.wikipedia.org/wiki/Visa_Inc.

[iii] Home Affordable Modification Program (HAMP): See link - http://makinghomeaffordable.gov/.

[iv] The Mortgage Forgiveness Debt Relief Act of 2007 and Debt Cancellation: See IRS.gov link - http://www.irs.gov/individuals/article/0,,id=179414,00.html

[v] The Bankruptcy Abuse Prevention and Consumer Protection Act of 2005: See link - http://en.wikipedia.org/wiki/Bankruptcy_Abuse_Prevention_and_Consumer_Protection_Act

[vi] *Investors Defaulting to Make Money* by Alex Ulam: See link -http://therealdeal.com/newyork/articles/defaulting-to-make-money

[vii] Four Seasons San Francisco in Default by J.K. Dineen: See link - http://sanfrancisco.bizjournals.com/sanfrancisco/stories/2009/07/06/daily68.html

---

[viii] Walk Away News: Morgan Stanley Gives Properties Back to the Lender by Emily Peck: See link - http://blogs.wsj.com/developments/2009/12/17/walk-away-news-morgan-stanley-gives-properties-back-to-the-lender/

[ix] Deutsche Bank Sues Trump by Zac Bissonnette: See link - http://www.bloggingstocks.com/2008/12/01/deutsche-bank-sues-donald-trump/

[x] *Mortgage Bankers Association Sells Headquarters at Big Loss* by James R. Hagerty. See Wall Street Journal link - http://online.wsj.com/article/SB10001424052748704829704575049111428912890.html

[xi] O The Mortgage Forgiveness Debt Relief Act of 2007 and Debt Cancellation: See IRS.gov link - http://www.irs.gov/individuals/article/0,,id=179414,00.html.

[xii] Underwater and Not Walking Away: Shame, Fear and the Social Management of the Housing Crises by Brent T. White.

[xiii] Fair Debt Collections Practices Act as amended in 2006: See link - http://www.ftc.gov/os/statutes/fdcpajump.shtm.

[xiv] Credit Card Accountability, Responsibility, and Disclosure Act of 2009.

[xv] A RESPA sample request letter template can be found on the U.S. Department of Housing and Urban Development (HUD) website www.hud.gov. See link - http://www.hud.gov/offices/hsg/ramh/res/reslettr.cfm.

[xvi] California's Rosenthal Fair Debt Collection Practices Act (Civil Code Section 1788-1788.3)

LaVergne, TN USA
19 November 2010
205548LV00005B/58/P

9 781609 104207